anything

D0515590

 anything

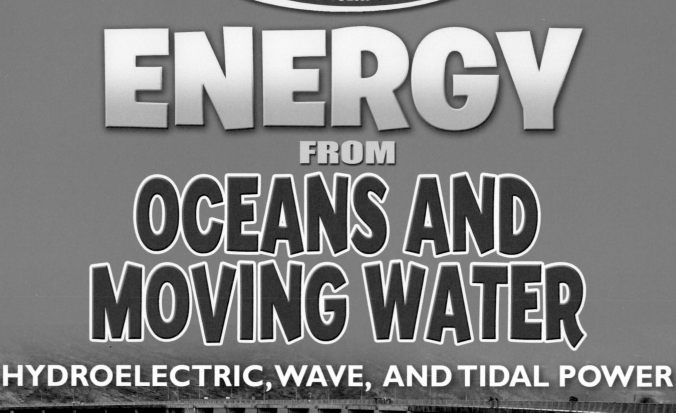

POWER
YESTERDAY • TODAY • TOMORROW

ENERGY
FROM
OCEANS AND
MOVING WATER

HYDROELECTRIC, WAVE, AND TIDAL POWER

by Ruth Owen

PowerKiDS press™

New York

Published in 2013 by The Rosen Publishing Group, Inc.
29 East 21st Street, New York, NY 10010

Produced for Rosen by Ruby Tuesday Books Ltd
Editor for Ruby Tuesday Books Ltd: Mark J. Sachner
US Editor: Sara Antill
Designer: Emma Randall
Consultant: Jeanine Gelhaus, M.S.; K-12 Energy Education Program, University of Wisconsin-Stevens Point

Photo Credits:
Cover, 1, 2–3, 4–5, 6–7, 8–9, 10–11, 12–13, 14–15, 18–19, 26–27, 28–29 © Shutterstock; 16–17 © Gregg M. Erickson, Wikipedia Creative Commons; 21 © Corbis; 22–23, 24–25 © Alamy; 25 (top) © Ocean Power Technologies, Wikipedia Creative Commons.

Publisher Cataloging Data

Owen, Ruth, 1967–
        Energy from oceans and moving water : hydroelectric, wave, and tidal power / by Ruth Owen.
p.   cm. — (Power: yesterday, today, tomorrow)
Includes index.
Summary: This book describes various ways electricity can be generated from water and the importance of finding renewable sources of power as fossil fuels run low and their use damages our planet.
Contents: Powering our world with water — Making electricity — Fossil fuels and climate change — Water power — From grinding grain to hydroelectric —A hydroelectric power station in action — Grand Coulee Dam — Helping fish bypass dams — The Three Gorges Dam — Harnessing tidal power — Harnessing wave power — Is water energy perfect power? — Water power for the future.
ISBN 978-1-4777-0269-7 (library binding) — ISBN 978-1-4777-0277-2 (pbk.) — ISBN 978-1-4777-0278-9 (6-pack)
        1. Water-power—Juvenile literature   [1. Water power   2. Renewable energy sources]   I. Title
                2013
        333.91/4—dc23

CONTENTS

Powering Our World with Water

If you've ever ridden on a white-water raft as it was carried down rapids by a torrent of rushing water, or stood at the ocean's edge as the sea pushed and pulled at your ankles, you've experienced the **energy** created by moving water.

As water flows down a river or rushes in and out at the shore, it is creating **kinetic energy**, or energy that is in motion. The kinetic energy in water can be captured and used to generate electricity. This type of electricity is known as hydroelectric power, or hydropower.

Around the world, scientists and engineers are working to find new and better ways to produce hydroelectric power. This is important work. Every day, more and more electricity is needed to run our modern world. Unfortunately, the main fuels we currently use to produce electricity are running out. Their use is also damaging Earth.

We need electricity, and we need it to be **renewable** and **environmentally friendly**. Is harnessing the energy in our planet's water the answer to powering our future?

White-water rafting is one way to feel the awesome power of water when it is in motion.

Some scientists estimate that if we could harness all the energy in ocean waves worldwide, we could produce enough electricity to power 100 planet Earths!

Making Electricity

Playing electric guitars and video games, using the Internet, and eating microwave popcorn are just a few of the fun things in life that require electricity. Add to the mix essential things such as air traffic control and life-saving equipment in hospitals, and it's clear to see that the world we know today couldn't exist without electricity.

When you flick on a switch, do you know how the electricity you are using got to your home, or what source of power was used to make it?

Electricity is generated in power stations. At a coal-fired power station, coal is burned inside huge boilers that heat water to such a high temperature that it becomes steam. Then the steam is used to spin giant **turbines**. The turbines power **generators**, which produce electricity.

In 2011, nearly 70 percent of the electricity generated in the United States was made by burning coal or **natural gas**. Now that's a big problem! Burning these fuels is harming the planet, and stocks of these fuels, buried deep inside Earth, are running low.

A coal-fired power station producing electricity

FAST FACT

*Electricity is measured in small units of power called watts. A **kilowatt-hour** (kWh) is a measure of energy that's the same as 1,000 watts working for one hour. For example, this would be the energy needed to light 25 40-watt lightbulbs for an hour. Every year in the United States, around 4,000,000,000,000 (4 trillion) kilowatt-hours of electricity are generated.*

Electricity is moved from power stations to homes, schools, and businesses through a network of power lines attached to transmission towers.

POWER SOURCES FOR US ELECTRICITY GENERATION IN 2011

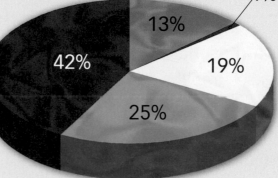

1%

13%

42%

19%

25%

 Renewable power sources, such as hydropower

Petroleum

Nuclear power

Natural gas

Coal

This chart shows the types of fuel or power sources used to generate electricity in the United States in 2011.

Fossil Fuels and Climate Change

Coal, natural gas, and oil have powered our world for decades. These fuels are known as **fossil fuels** because they formed from the remains of ancient animals and plants.

Fossil fuels are **nonrenewable**. They took millions of years to form, so we cannot make more when they are all used up, and that time is approaching fast!

The burning of fossil fuels is also damaging our planet. When fossil fuels are burned, to make electricity, for example, gases such as carbon dioxide, methane, and nitrous oxide are released into the Earth's **atmosphere**. Known as **greenhouse gases**, these gases trap the Sun's heat on Earth, just as a greenhouse traps heat inside. This has led to a gradual increase in Earth's temperatures that is leading to **climate change**.

We need heat on Earth, but too much is harmful. Warmer temperatures will cause ocean levels to rise because water expands when it is heated. This could cause low-lying coastal places to flood. In other places, the climate will become so hot and dry that water supplies will disappear and people will have trouble growing food.

Climate change may cause drought. This is when no rain (or less rain than usual) falls for months or even years.

Warmer temperatures will cause ice at the North and South poles to melt.

FAST FACT

Oil, natural gas, and coal formed when plants and animals died and their remains settled on the ocean floor and at the bottom of swamps.

The remains were buried by layers of soil or water.

Over millions of years, heat and pressure turned the remains to oil, natural gas, and coal that we extract from deep underground.

300 to 400 million years ago

Ocean

300 to 400 million years ago

50 to 100 million years ago

Ocean

Layers of sand and soil

Animal remains

50 to 100 million years ago

Water

Layers of soil

Dead Plants

Today

Oil drilling rig

Ocean

Land

Gas

Layers of soil and rock

Oil

Today

Layers of soil and rock

Coal

Mine

Water Power

Today, with fossil fuels running out and damaging our planet, we need renewable, environmentally-friendly ways to generate electricity.

One option is to use the kinetic energy in water to turn turbines that power generators to produce electricity. Making electricity in this way creates no greenhouse gases.

Water Power: Rivers and Dams

Water power can be harnessed by using a **dam** on a river. A dam is a structure that blocks the river. Water builds up behind the dam in a large lake, or **reservoir**. When water is released through the dam from the reservoir, it flows at high speed past turbines and spins them.

Tidal Power

Spend a day on a beach, and you will notice that the **tide** comes in and out. In just a few hours, millions of gallons of water may flow into a bay and then out again. This moving water can be used to turn turbines.

Wave Power

As wind moves over water, it creates waves. A wave is packed with kinetic energy that can be used to power turbines.

Water drops gather together and form rain clouds. In very cold air, water drops may freeze and become snow.

The Water Cycle

Water vapor rises high into the sky where it is cold. The vapor condenses and forms water drops.

Rain and snow fall from clouds back to Earth.

Water on Earth is warmed by the Sun. It evaporates and becomes a gas called water vapor.

Rainwater and melted snow runs into rivers, which eventually run into the ocean.

From Grinding Grain to Hydroelectric

Using water as a source of energy is not a new idea. Civilizations, such as the ancient Greeks, were using water to drive water wheels, a very simple kind of turbine, over 2,000 years ago.

A large wooden wheel would be placed vertically in moving water such as a stream. As the water flowed over the blades, or paddle-like attachments, around the outside of the wheel, it caused the wheel to spin. The water wheel then turned an **axle**, which could drive any combination of gears and wheels in other machines. For centuries, water wheels powered machines for tasks such as grinding grain into flour and cutting timber in sawmills.

FAST FACT

The Appleton power station was set up by a paper manufacturer named H. J. Rogers. A water wheel was used to drive the generator, which produced enough electricity to run the power station and to power Rogers' house and two papermills.

In the late 1800s, water, or hydro, power began to be used to produce electricity. In 1882, the world's first hydroelectric power station began operating in Appleton, Wisconsin. In the early days of hydropower, the electricity produced could only be used close to the water source. As the technology to transmit electricity over longer distances improved, however, more people could benefit from this new type of power.

A traditional water wheel

Blade or paddle

Axle

A Hydroelectric Power Station in Action

Since the early days of hydroelectric power in Appleton, Wisconsin, thousands of hydroelectric power stations have been built worldwide. Today, large power stations can produce billions of kilowatt-hours of electricity every year. So what actually happens inside a hydroelectric power station?

A dam is built across a river and holds back the water to create a reservoir. When gates on the dam open, gravity pulls water from the reservoir toward turbines through large pipes, called penstocks. The water strikes the turbines' blades, causing them to spin. The turbines are attached to generators. As the turbines spin, it makes magnets inside the generators rotate past coils of copper wire, which produce electricity.

Once through the turbines, the water flows along pipelines called spillways that deliver the water back into the river on the other side of the dam. No harmful greenhouse gases have been produced, and the water is back where it started in the river, ready to play its part in Earth's water cycle!

FAST FACT

The Hoover Dam was built on the Colorado River in the 1930s. Inside the dam's hydroelectric power station, water from the river drives 17 main turbines to produce 4 billion kilowatt-hours of electricity each year.

Turbines at the Hoover Dam hydroelectric power station

Hoover Dam

Reservoir

The base of the massive Hoover Dam is as thick as two football fields laid end to end.

Hydroelectric power station

Grand Coulee Dam

About 29 percent of the hydroelectric power produced in the United States each year comes from the state of Washington. That's because Washington is home to the Grand Coulee Dam, the nation's largest dam and hydroelectric power station.

Situated on the Columbia River, the Grand Coulee Dam is 550 feet (168 m) high and 5,223 feet (1,683 m) long. If the concrete inside the dam was used to build a highway, the highway would stretch from Seattle, Washington to Miami, Florida!

The Grand Coulee Dam on the Columbia River, in Washington

The Grand Coulee Dam power station supplies electricity to 11 US states and Canada. Each year, it generates 21 billion kilowatt-hours of electricity. That's enough to power 2.3 million homes.

The reservoir, or lake, behind the dam is named Franklin D. Roosevelt Lake, or Lake Roosevelt. It was named for President Roosevelt who was in office during the construction of the dam in the 1930s. The lake covers an area that's larger than 75,000 football fields, end zone to end zone!

FAST FACT

The land that is now beneath the waters of Lake Roosevelt was once home to 11 towns. Residents of the towns were moved to new places, and the towns' buildings were burned or dismantled. Then the whole area was flooded as the new lake formed behind the dam.

Helping Fish Bypass Dams

Hydroelectric power may be renewable and "green," but building dams can disrupt the natural behavior and life cycles of fish that live in a river.

After hatching in their spawning, or breeding, grounds, many types of fish swim for the ocean, following the river downstream. Years later, as adults, they swim back upstream to breed at the place where they were born. Builders of dams have to find ways to help migrating fish bypass a dam.

Jumping up a fish ladder is no problem for a salmon, as the fish will jump natural obstacles, such as waterfalls, as it swims upstream.

FAST FACT

In some places, fish elevators help adult fish get over dams. Fish swim into a large, water-filled "elevator," or box, at the base of the dam. The elevator then rises and delivers the fish into a water flume that carries them back into the river on the other side of the dam.

At the Rocky Reach Dam on the Columbia River in Washington, young fish swimming downstream are encouraged by water currents to enter a wide steel tube. The fish swim along the tube, which passes through the dam and then safely delivers them on the other side further downstream.

When adult fish encounter a dam on their journey upstream, they can be helped by the construction of a fish ladder. The ladder is a series of connected pools. The fish jump from pool to pool, slowly making their way up the ladder, which takes them around the dam and back to the river further upstream.

A fish ladder bypassing a dam

The Three Gorges Dam

Completed in 2012, the Three Gorges Dam on the Yangtze River in China is the world's largest and most controversial dam and hydroelectric power station.

Built to hold back waters that can cause devastating floods farther down the river, the dam is also an important source of energy. The Three Gorges Dam has the capacity to generate around 10 percent of China's electricity. That's enough to power over 18 million homes.

This all sounds very positive, but many people including scientists, environmentalists, and human rights activists have serious concerns about the project.

The dam was built on two major **fault lines**. There is some evidence that changes in pressure on the land as vast quantities of water enter and empty from the reservoir could actually cause an earthquake.

Pollution in the 400-mile-(644 km) long reservoir, a major source of drinking water, is also a huge concern. Beneath the reservoir's waters are the remains of cities, towns, and hundreds of villages. Homes, factories, mines, and waste dumps were simply flooded as the reservoir filled, without any of the waste being removed.

FAST FACT

Over 1.2 million people were ordered by the Chinese government to leave their homes so that the Three Gorges Dam could be built. Many people received little or no help to relocate.

Billions of tons (t) of sewage and trash are dumped or washed into the Yangtze River every year. Here, trash and other waste is trapped in the reservoir behind the Three Gorges Dam.

Flood waters are released in a controlled way through the Three Gorges Dam following a period of high flood waters in July 2012.

Harnessing Tidal Power

Just like rivers, ocean waters present opportunities for making electricity.

Every 24 hours, most coastlines experience two high tides (when the ocean comes in) and two low tides (when it goes out). One way to harness the energy in all this moving water is to build a dam, known as a barrage, across a bay, **estuary**, or harbor. As the tide moves in and out through the barrage, water flows over turbines that power generators. For a barrage to be effective, the difference between a low and high tide must be at least 16 feet (5 m) to ensure enough water flows in and out.

Another way to harness tidal power is to place giant turbines—which look like the wind turbines we see on land—underwater in an area offshore where there are powerful tides. As tidal water surges past a turbine, its rotors spin and power a generator.

Around the world, scientists and engineers are developing and testing tidal power equipment. Compared to hydroelectric power, this technology is still in its early stages.

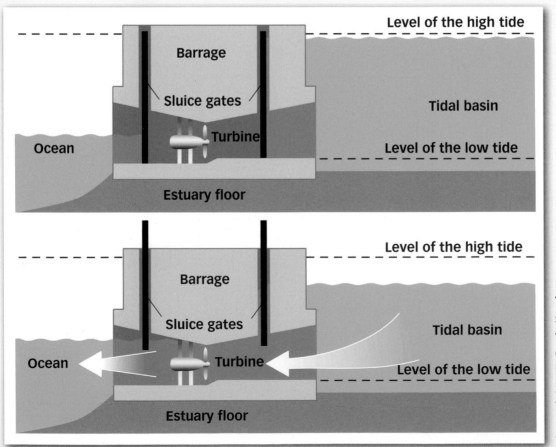

Tidal barrages open sluice gates to let tidal water into an estuary, or tidal basin. As the tide goes out, the water flows over the barrage's turbines to create power.

The AK1000, exhibited here on land, is just one of many tidal turbines in development. The turbine is 74 feet (22.5 m) tall and can generate electricity to power 1,000 homes.

Rotor

Harnessing Wave Power

Wave power uses the natural energy in waves to produce electricity. There will always be waves, so this type of power is renewable.

Like tidal power, this type of technology is in its early stages and many different ways of harnessing wave energy are under development. Some wave power devices are anchored to the seabed, while others float on the water. Most designs feature a moving part fixed to a stationary part. Like a piston in a car's engine, the moving part moves up and down with the motion of the waves. This piston-like action pressurizes air or oil inside the device to drive a turbine.

The PB150 Power Buoy, shown on land in Scotland, is designed to float in the ocean. Waves move fluid within the buoy to spin a generator. The device is 145 feet (44 m) tall.

FAST FACT

Wave power devices are very expensive to develop. Once they are operational, however, they cost very little to run. Wave power creates no greenhouse gases, but liquids, such as oil, used inside the equipment could leak and pollute the sea harming ocean animals and plants.

Wave Hub is a test facility in the Atlantic Ocean 10 miles (16 km) off the coast of Cornwall, England. Here, companies developing wave power devices can rent an area of the ocean to test their equipment. Wave power machines can be "plugged into" a shared hub that then transmits the electricity to the UK's power grid through a 15.5-mile-(25 km) long underwater cable.

The PB150 Power Buoy floating in the ocean

Is Water Energy Perfect Power?

To combat climate change, we must stop burning fossil fuels to make electricity. We also need to generate electricity using energy sources that are renewable.

Water is a renewable energy source, and using it to make electricity creates no greenhouse gases. These are the two major benefits of using hydropower, but what are the others? And are there any downsides to using energy from water?

Hydropower Pros

✓ Dams are not only used to produce hydroelectric power. At times when there is excessive rainfall and a danger of flooding, they hold back river water to stop floods from happening further downstream.

✓ Many countries may not have natural stocks of fossil fuels and have to buy them from other countries. If these countries have ocean water or places where they can build dams, they can use hydropower to generate their own electricity.

✓ Reservoirs are places where people can enjoy leisure activities such as swimming, fishing, sailing, and water sports.

✓ The water collected in reservoirs behind dams can supply water to nearby towns and cities and irrigate farmland.

✓ Wind and solar power rely on the wind blowing and the Sun shining, which can be unpredictable. The ocean's tides can reliably be predicted, however. The direction in which waves will move is also predictable.

✓ Micro hydroelectric power plants can be set up on a small waterway to supply electricity to a village, farm, or a single home.

Hydropower Cons

X Dams are hugely expensive and time-consuming to build. Many of the best places to locate hydroelectric power stations have already been used.

X Building a dam can change a river's water levels, flow patterns, or temperature. This can disrupt the lives of wild animals and damage plant life. Large structures, such as barrages or floating wave power devices, can disrupt the lives of ocean animals.

X In order to build a dam and create a reservoir, thousands of people may lose their homes. Wildlife habitats could also be lost.

X The large quantity of water collected in a reservoir may emit greenhouse gases. Scientists are still studying if the level of gases is harmful.

X A hydroelectric power station depends on rain and snow falling in order to keep the river flowing and the reservoir supplied with water. The amounts of rain and snow that fall cannot be controlled.

X Over time, wave and tidal power equipment can suffer wear and tear from the pounding of the ocean. This can be difficult and expensive to repair.

This beautiful torrent of rushing water contains the energy to power homes, schools, stores, and factories.

Water Power for the Future

Over 70 percent of our Earth is covered with water. This means there's a massive amount of water energy on our planet that can be used to make electricity.

On the whole, electricity production using hydroelectric power stations has been a big success story. In the future, there may not be the space available to build more Hoover Dams or Grand Coulee Dams. The technology could be used, however, to build small power stations capable of supplying electricity to a single community.

Right now, it's proving expensive to produce electricity using wave and tidal power. It can cost up to 16 cents to produce a kilowatt-hour of electricity using wave power. This compares to just 3 cents for electricity from a coal-fired power station. Work is going on worldwide, though, to develop technologies that will make wave and tidal power more cost-effective and viable.

Our amazing planet gave us water for drinking, producing food, and using for fun. Now, it's time to find as many ways as possible to use this fantastic natural resource to power our world and keep it clean and safe for the future.

Scientists have estimated that if all the wave power off the coastline of the United States was harnessed, it could generate enough electricity to supply about 6 percent of the nation's electricity needs!

Glossary

atmosphere (AT-muh-sfeer)
The layer of gases surrounding a planet, moon, or star.

axle (AK-sul)
A shaft on or with which a wheel rotates. Also, a rod connecting a pair of wheels on a vehicle.

climate change (KLY-mut CHAYNJ)
The gradual change in temperatures on Earth. For example, the current warming of temperatures caused by a buildup of greenhouse gases in the atmosphere.

dam (DAM)
A barrier built across moving water to hold back and raise the level of the water, often to create a reservoir.

energy (EH-ner-jee)
The ability to do work.

environmentally friendly
(in-vy-run-MENT-tul-ee FREND-lee)
Not damaging or polluting to the natural world.

estuary (ES-choo-wer-ee)
A body of water on a coastline that has one or more rivers or streams flowing into it.

fault line (FAWLT LYN)
A large crack in the crust, or rocky outer layer, of the Earth.

fossil fuels (FO-sul FYOOLZ)
Fuels that formed over millions of years from the remains of plants and animals. Oil, natural gas, and coal are all fossil fuels.

generator (JEH-neh-ray-tur)
A machine that turns mechanical energy, for example the spinning of a turbine, into electrical energy.

greenhouse gases
(GREEN-hows GAS-ez)
Gases such as carbon dioxide, methane, and nitrous oxide that occur naturally and are also released into Earth's atmosphere when fossil fuels are burned.

kilowatt-hour (KIH-luh-waht-ow-er)
A measure of energy that's the same as 1,000 watts working for one hour. A watt is a small unit of power.

kinetic energy
(kuh-NEH-tik EH-ner-jee)
Energy that is in motion. Wind and moving water are two sources of kinetic energy.

natural gas (NA-chuh-rul GAS)
A fossil fuel that formed underground over millions of years. It is piped to homes and businesses to be used as a source of energy.

nonrenewable (non-ree-NOO-uh-bul)
A resource, such as coal, that cannot be renewed once it is used.

renewable (ree-NOO-uh-bul)
A resource that can be produced again and again and will not run out.

reservoir (REH-zuh-vwar)
A large natural or artificial lake where water is collected to be used as drinking water or to power a hydroelectric power station.

tide (TYD)
The rising and falling of water in an ocean, sea, or large lake.

turbine (TER-byn)
A machine with a wheel or rotor that turns and generates power. A turbine can be driven by gas, water, or steam.

water cycle (WAH-ter SY-kul)
The process in which water evaporates and moves from Earth up into the sky as water vapor, condenses into water drops to form clouds, and falls back to Earth again as rain or snow.

WEBSITES

Due to the changing nature of Internet links, PowerKids Press has developed an online list of websites related to the subject of this book. This site is updated regularly. Please use this link to access the list:

www.powerkidslinks.com/pytt/hydro/

Read More

Hansen, Amy S. *Hydropower: Making a Splash!.* Powering Our World. New York: PowerKids Press, 2010.

Rodger, Marguerite. *Hydroelectric Power: Power from Moving Water.* Energy Revolution. New York: Crabtree Publishing, 2010.

Webster, Christine. *Water Power.* Water Science. New York: Weigl Publishing, 2011.

Index

A
AK1000 tidal turbine, 23
Appleton power station, 12–13

B
barrages, 22, 27
biomass power, 29

C
carbon dioxide, 8
climate change, 8, 26
coal, 6–9
coal-fired power stations, 6, 28
Colorado River, 14
Columbia River, 16, 19

E
electricity, 4–8, 10, 12–14, 16–17, 20, 22–26, 28–29

F
fault lines, 20
fish, 18–19
fish ladders, 18–19
fossil fuels, 8–10, 26
Franklin D. Roosevelt Lake, 17

G
generators, 6, 10, 12, 14, 22, 24
geothermal power, 29
Grand Coulee Dam, 16–17, 28
greenhouse gases, 8, 10, 14, 24, 26–27

H
habitats, 27
Hoover Dam, 14–15, 28
hydroelectric power, 4, 7, 12–13, 22, 26–27, 29
hydroelectric power stations, 12–17, 20, 27–28

K
kilowatt-hours (kWhs), 7, 14, 17, 28
kinetic energy, 4, 10

M
methane, 8

N
natural gas, 6–9
nitrous oxide, 8
nuclear power, 7

O
oceans, 4–5, 8–9, 11, 18, 22, 24–27
oil, 8–9, 24

P
PB150 Power Buoy, 24–25
penstocks, 14
petroleum, 7
pipeline, 14
pollution, 20–21, 24
power lines, 7

R
rain, 8, 11, 26–27
reservoirs, 10, 14–15, 17, 20–21, 26–27
rivers, 4, 10–11, 14, 18–19, 22, 26–27
Rocky Reach Dam, 19

S
snow, 11, 27
solar power, 26, 29
spillways, 14
steam, 6

T
Three Gorges Dam, 20–21
tidal power, 10, 22–24, 27–28
tidal turbines, 22–23
tides, 10, 22, 26
transmission towers, 7
turbines, 6, 10, 12, 14–15, 22–24

W
water cycle, 11, 14
water wheels, 12–13
Wave Hub, 25
wave power, 10, 24–25, 27–29
waves, 5, 10, 24, 26
wind power, 26, 29

Y
Yangtze River, 20–21